WEIRD!

The Complete Book of Halloween Words

By Peter R. Limburg

Pictures By Betsy Lewin

BRADBURY PRESS
NEW YORK

Bradbury Press
An Affiliate of Macmillan, Inc.
866 Third Avenue, New York, NY 10022
Collier Macmillan Canada, Inc.
First Edition
Printed and bound in the United States of America
10 9 8 7 6 5 4 3 2 1
Book design by Julie Quan

LIBRARY OF CONGRESS CATALOGING-IN-PUBLICATION DATA
Limburg, Peter R.
Weird! : the complete book of Halloween words / by
Peter R. Limburg ; illustrated by Betsy Lewin.
p. cm.
Bibliography: p.
Includes index.
Summary: Presents definitions and the historical background of
words associated with Halloween.
ISBN 0-02-759050-X
1. Halloween—Dictionaries, Juvenile. [1. Halloween—
Dictionaries.] I. Lewin, Betsy, ill. II. Title.
GT4965.L39 1989
394.2′683—dc19   88-38678 CIP AC

In honor of all those who have upheld
knowledge and truth, and battled
ignorance, superstition, and the
narrow minds of censors.

CONTENTS

HALLOWEEN is celebrated on the thirty-first of OCTOBER.

HALLOWEEN

Although Halloween means ghosts, goblins, witches, jack-o'-lanterns, and trick or treat to most of us, the name itself really comes from a special religious festival honoring saints. As far back as the eighth century A.D., the Catholic church decreed that the first of November should be All Saints' Day. In English this day came to be called All Hallows' Day, and the night before it was All Hallows' Eve, or All Hallows' E'en. In time this became shortened to Hallowe'en. The name "Hallowe'en" first appeared around the middle of the sixteenth century, and we have been using it ever since. Nowadays it is spelled without the apostrophe.

Do you wonder how the fun and playful spookiness of Halloween got mixed up with a solemn occasion like All Saints' Day? Here's the story.

Many centuries ago, long before the Christian era, a group of people called the Celts (see the TIMELINE) occupied a large part of Europe, stretching from Spain all the way east to the Black Sea. They also inhabited the British Isles. For the Celts, the end of October and beginning of November marked the end of the year.

Summer was over. The crops had been harvested weeks earlier, and it was time to bring the cattle and sheep in from the pastures. The sun was about to go into hiding for the winter—a dread time of cold and dark. Fittingly, the ancient Celts celebrated the first of November as the Day of the Dead. So did many other peoples of pre-Christian Europe.

🦉 Do You Know

Saints and *hallows* really mean the same thing. *Saint* comes from the Latin *sanctus*, meaning "holy." *Hallow* and *holy* both come from an old Germanic root that carried the idea of something that must be kept *whole*, that is, protected from any injury.

E'en is a short form of *even*, the word that English speakers over a thousand years ago used to mean the end of daylight. They had another word, *evening*, which meant the coming on of "even." So Hallowe'en really means "holy evening" or "saints' evening."

In the old days, people marked the passage of the year by the festivals and fasts of the Church. Until the sixteenth century, the Catholic church ruled supreme in most of Europe, from Spain in the west to Poland and Hungary in the east, and from Italy in the south to Norway in the north. When people spoke of the Church, it was the Roman Catholic church they meant.

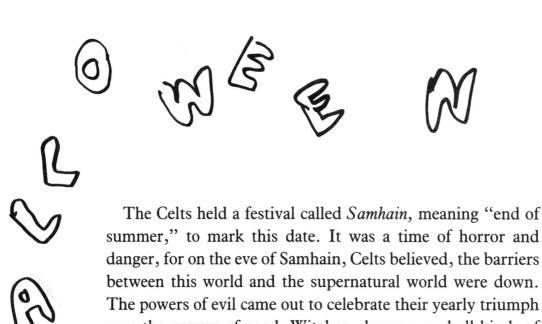

The Celts held a festival called *Samhain,* meaning "end of summer," to mark this date. It was a time of horror and danger, for on the eve of Samhain, Celts believed, the barriers between this world and the supernatural world were down. The powers of evil came out to celebrate their yearly triumph over the powers of good. Witches, demons, and all kinds of other evil creatures rampaged freely until dawn. The souls of the dead, too, came back to visit the living. Sometimes they sought revenge for wrongs that had been done to them during their lifetimes.

Samhain was the most important festival of the year for the pagan Celts. On the eve of Samhain, priests lit huge bonfires (from "bone fire") to frighten off the raging demons, witches, and ghosts. In Ireland all the fires in the land were put out before sunset, and the chief priest lit a new fire. From this one sacred flame, all the household fires in Ireland were re-kindled.

According to a medieval Irish document, the priests burned live children on the Samhain fire to gain the favor of the gods they worshiped. The chief god, called Cromm Cruach, was bloodthirsty and dangerous. Irish legend tells how he destroyed the very king who taught the people to worship him!

There were other rituals to perform on Samhain for the sake of safety and well-being. People put out sweets and other good things to eat to placate the evil spirits and keep them from doing harm. Some, hoping to fool the demons, disguised themselves as evil spirits and roamed the countryside, committing malicious pranks, until dawn sent the ghosts and devils back to their unholy realm.

It is almost certain that the Church chose the first of November to be All Saints' Day to make the people of Europe, most of whom had not been Christian for very long, forget about the old pagan festival of Samhain. But these new Christians, although they went to church and said their prayers, did not forget. The old beliefs and the old fears lived on, and so did many of the old rituals.

People continued to light ritual fires, for example. They continued to roam about in disguises, making mischief. And they continued to offer the demons and ghosts delicacies to eat—though over the course of the centuries they took to eating these goodies themselves, and Halloween became not a dreaded vigil but an occasion for fun.

OCTOBER

October is the tenth month of our year. But the word *October* comes from the Latin *octobris mensis*, meaning "eighth month." This is because the old Roman year began in March, the time when farmers did their spring plowing and planted the grain they would harvest in the fall.

Unfortunately, the Roman priests, who controlled the calendar because religious festivals depended on it, did not administer it properly. They fiddled with dates in order to prolong the terms in office of politicians who were their allies, or to make election days come at a time that would favor their friends. So by the first century B.C., the official calendar was three months out of step with the real year. The months that were supposed to be winter months came in the fall, the spring months fell in the middle of winter, and the autumn months came in summer! To end this confusion, Julius Caesar, the

popular and powerful dictator of Rome, reformed the calendar in 46 B.C. In the process, he decreed that the New Year would henceforth begin on January 1. This made October the tenth month, but Caesar kept its old name.

The Anglo-Saxons called October *Winter-fylleth* (winter full moon), because they considered that winter began with the October full moon, one of the turning points of the year. The ancient Celtic festival of Samhain, from which so much of our Halloween lore is derived, was also timed to coincide with the end of October.

Do You Know

Ancient Rome was not the only place where the new year began in March. France clung to a New Year's date of March 1 until 1564; Scotland hung on until 1599; while England did not officially change over to January 1 until 1752!

Julius Caesar's idea of changing the New Year from March to January made pretty good sense. It brought the New Year close to the winter solstice, when the days at last stopped growing shorter and the daylight began to return. It also coincided conveniently with a riotous holiday season called the *Saturnalia*, a faint memory of which lingers on in our New Year's Eve celebrations.

So you want to go TRICK-OR-TREATING?
Be prepared for a SPOOKY,
SCARY, GRUESOME, EERIE,
and WEIRD night!

TRICK OR TREAT

Trick-or-treating became popular in the United States toward the end of the nineteenth century. It was probably brought here by Irish immigrants who came to the New World to seek a better life. In Ireland it was an ancient custom for peasants to beg from house to house on Halloween in order to get together enough food or money for a feast. If the people of the house were stingy, the beggars threatened to call down the wrath of the saints.

Another origin of trick-or-treating may be the English custom of "souling." People went about on All Saints' Day (November 1) and All Souls' Day (November 2) begging for "soul cakes," which were square currant buns made in remembrance of the dead. In return, the beggars promised to say extra prayers for the souls of the dead family members.

Some historians think that trick-or-treating originated in the Guy Fawkes Day celebration of England, on November 5, when people dragged scarecrowlike figures of the executed traitor Guy Fawkes through the streets. They set fire to the effigies while the children capered about, screeching and begging for "A penny for the Old Guy!"

It is possible that all three of these customs blended into the American one.

The word *trick* comes from the Old French *trique*, meaning a stratagem for deceiving or cheating. In the sense of a malicious prank, it dates from the late sixteenth century. You will find it in more than one of William Shakespeare's plays: "Didst thou ever see me do such a trick?" (*Two Gentlemen of Verona*, Act IV, Scene 4, line 43); "Or I shall break that merry sconce of yours / That stands on tricks when I am undisposed." (*A Comedy of Errors*, Act I, Scene 2, lines 79–80). *Trick* is one of those Shakespearean words that does not need to be translated into modern English—unlike *sconce*, which now means a wall fixture that holds a light bulb, but in Shakespeare's day meant a lantern. In the play, Shakespeare uses it as a slangy way of saying "head."

Treat has a more complicated story. The Romans had a word, *tractare*, which meant "to drag." In time, the word took on the meaning of negotiating. These negotiations were usually dragged out to great lengths as each person argued and tried to get the better of the other over the details. This was the sense in which it first appeared in English, shortly before the fourteenth century. An English lord could have said to the neighboring lord, "Let us treat about where my domain ends and yours begins." If he were lucky, the neighboring lord would agree. Otherwise he might have a local war on his hands.

In less than a hundred years, which is a pretty short time in the development of a language, people were also using *treat* to mean dealing with other people or with animals. So before 1400 you could have said, "Sir John's ghost treats me coldly when it appears."

Though it began as a verb, *treat* also became a noun. In the sense of something nice that you get for free, particularly something to eat or drink, it goes back as far as the mid-seventeenth century. Back then, you could give a friend a treat such as a mug of ale or an orange (a costly luxury imported from a Mediterranean land). But you could not have treated your friend to a spooky movie, because movies had not been invented yet.

SPOOKY

Spooky is a gift to us from the Dutch. *Spook* is a Dutch word for "ghost," and early Dutch settlers brought the word with them to America in the seventeenth century. The Dutch colonists enlivened many an evening with spook stories. In time, English-speaking colonists picked up *spook* along with other Dutch words such as *coleslaw*, *boss*, and *cookie*. To make it an adjective, they simply added a *y* at the end, the way we made *jumpy* from *jump*.

In Brittany, a region in the northwest of France where ancient Celtic tradition runs strong, children used to hide in graveyards on Halloween and wave skulls with lighted candles inside at anyone who happened to walk by. What a spooky sight!

SCARY

Scary and *scare* come from an Old Norse word, *skiarr*, that meant "timid." English speakers probably learned it from the Vikings, who sailed from their homes in Norway and Denmark and raided and plundered all of western Europe in the eighth and ninth centuries A.D.

The English, and many other peoples, regarded the Vikings as devils in human form. One old English prayer ran, "From the fury of the Northmen, deliver us, O Lord!" The sight of a long, slender Viking ship on the horizon, with its dragon-headed prow and its big, striped sail, was almost as terrifying as the vision of an attacking monster! But in time the Vikings settled down in many of the places they had raided, such as the east of England. And in time they blended in with the rest of the population; many of their words passed into the English language, including *sky, window, egg, husband*, and, of course, *scary*.

GRUESOME

Gruesome is a perfect word for describing devils and witches and the ghosts you might find in a graveyard, for it comes from an old Scottish verb, *grue*, that meant "to feel horror" or the natural result of feeling horror, "to shudder." In the old days *grue* was often spelled *grow*, for people could not agree on how it should be pronounced.

At some point during the Middle Ages, the ending *some* was tacked on to make an adjective, just as we have added a *y* to *scare* to make *scary*. But *gruesome* remained a provincial word until Sir Walter Scott (1771–1832), a romantic-minded Scotsman who became one of the first best-selling authors, used it in his novel *Old Mortality* in 1816. Even then, Scott spelled it differently; he spelled it *grewsome*. Authors of Gothic novels found the word useful, but the modern spelling did not take hold until after 1850.

The Gothic novel was invented in England before the American Revolution. The first one was published in 1764. A Gothic novel is a scary tale that combines generous portions of horror, supernatural effects, violence, and death. The early Gothic novels were written in high-flown, elegant language, and they were set in gloomy, picturesque surroundings such as old, crumbling castles. In fact, they got the name "Gothic" because the castles and other buildings that the authors loved to describe were built in the Gothic style.

Some famous Gothic novels are *The Castle of Otranto*, by Horace Walpole (1764); *Vathek*, by William Beckford (1786); *The Monk*, by Matthew Gregory Lewis (1796)—and, of course, *Frankenstein*, by Mary Wollstonecraft Shelley (1818).

Americans also loved Gothic novels. One pioneer American Gothic writer was Nathaniel Hawthorne (1804–1864), who drew on the shuddery legends of his hometown of Salem, Massachusetts. (One of his ancestors was a judge in the notorious Salem witch trials.) Another famous Gothic writer—with a very morbid imagination—was Edgar Allan Poe (1809–1849). Some of Poe's short stories, such as "The Fall of the House of Usher," "The Masque of the Red Death," and "The Pit and the Pendulum," are classic Gothic horror tales.

EERIE

Argh! No, this time we don't mean the familiar exclamation of characters in the comic strips, but the old, old word from which *eerie* is descended. *Argh*, or its alternate form *earg*, was an Old English word that meant "cowardly" or "fearful."

By the beginning of the fourteenth century, people were spelling the word *eri* and pronouncing it about the way we do today. Although the spelling changed, it still kept the meaning of "fearful." Gradually, it picked up a flavor of supernatural dread, too.

But in the late eighteenth century *eerie* did a flip-flop. Instead of describing the way people felt ("The cracked, hideous voice of the old witch-woman and her wildly rolling eyes make me eerie"), it came to describe the things that gave them the spooky feelings of dread and foreboding ("The moldering skeleton, a rusty dagger still clutched in its grip, was an eerie sight"). This is the sense in which we use it today. The old meaning lingers on, however, especially in Scotland, and people can still say things such as, "This damp, gloomy forest with its mysterious noises gives me an eerie feeling."

Eerie is one of the favorite words of horror-story writers. In the hands of a skillful author, this word can make a reader's skin crawl. A good word to think of when you are trick-or-treating on Halloween!

WEIRD

Like *eerie, weird* is one of those words that is meant to send shivers down your spine. *Weird* comes from the Old English word *wyrd*, which was a noun and meant "fate" or "destiny." Later, it also came to mean magical power or someone who had magical power, such as a witch or wizard.

Apparently it was Shakespeare who first used *weird* as an adjective, in his famous play *Macbeth* (1605). In Act I, Scene 3, the three witches chant: "The weird sisters, hand in hand, / Posters of the sea and land, / Thus do go about, about, . . ."

In a later scene the weird sisters brew a sinister potion as they recite a charm.

First Witch. Round about the cauldron go:
In the poisoned entrails throw.
Toad, that under cold stone
Days and nights has thirty-one
Swelter'd venom sleeping got,
Boil thou first i' the charmed pot.

All. Double, double toil and trouble;
Fire burn and cauldron bubble.

Second Witch. Fillet of a fenny snake,
In the cauldron boil and bake;
Eye of newt and toe of frog,
Wool of bat and tongue of dog,
Adder's fork and blind-worm's sting,
Lizard's leg and howlet's wing,
For a charm of powerful trouble,
Like a hell-broth boil and bubble.

All. Double, double toil and trouble;
Fire burn and cauldron bubble.

Third Witch. Scale of dragon, tooth of wolf,
Witches' mummy, maw and gulf
of the ravin'd salt-sea shark,
Root of hemlock digg'd i' the dark; . . .

Second Witch. Cool it with a baboon's blood,
Then the charm is firm and good. . . .
By the pricking of my thumbs,
Something wicked this way comes:
Open, locks,
Whoever knocks!

William Shakespeare. *Macbeth*, Act IV, Scene 1.

Shakespeare's plays were so popular that the new use of *weird* caught on. As Shakespeare used the word, *weird* meant "having the power to control the fate of a person."

About two hundred years later Percy Bysshe Shelley (1792–1822), a young English romantic poet, expanded the meaning to include anything suggestive of the supernatural or of an uncanny nature. For example, in a long poem called "Alastor" (1815), he wrote, "In lone and silent hours, / When night makes a weird sound of its own stillness. . . ."

Shelley and his poet friend John Keats (1795–1821) also popularized the sense of *weird* as meaning "bizarre" or "odd," which is the way most young people use it today. In "Alastor," Shelley writes of "weird clouds," and Keats, in his poem "Lamia" (1819), tells of a nymph who drenches her hair in "weird syrops" to make herself invisible and escape the unwanted attentions of amorous gods.

So think about Shakespeare, Shelley, and Keats the next time you call that oddball in the fifth grade *weird*!

Try taking the shortcut
through the GRAVEYARD,
past TOMBSTONES
and between COFFINS. It's
MIDNIGHT, and the MOON is full.
Beware, you will probably see
a SKELETON and a SKULL, an OWL,
a BAT, a CAT, a DEVIL, and
an IMP pulling a PRANK
on a GOBLIN and GHOST.

KICK
ME

ME
TOO

GRAVEYARD

Grave comes from the Old English word *grafan*, "to dig," and refers to the pit or trench that is dug in the ground to hold a corpse. *Yard* comes from the Old English *geard*, meaning "fence" or "dwelling." Put them together, and you have *graveyard*. And every proper graveyard does have a fence or a wall around it.

Cemetery is a synonym for graveyard. Our English word comes from the Latin term *caemeterium*, but the Romans got that word from the Greek *koimeterion*, which literally means a dormitory. (A dormitory is a place where a number of people sleep, as in a college dormitory.)

In Europe in the Middle Ages, graveyards became so crowded that bodies had to be dug up after a few years to make room for new ones. Important people arranged to have themselves buried inside the churches, in graves right under the church floor or in caskets placed along the wall. Being buried inside the church insured that your bones would not be dug up and thrown away. Some churches had special underground chambers, called crypts, where very important people were buried. You can still see these indoor graves in old churches in Europe.

Although many Americans and Europeans consider graveyards to be scary places, especially on Halloween, Mexican families take picnic lunches to the cemetery on All Hallows' Day, or the Day of the Dead (November 1), and celebrate the festival by the graves of their loved ones so that the dead can join in the fun!

🦉 Do You Know

In the nineteenth century many people were afraid of being buried alive. For these nervous souls, clever inventors patented several types of coffins fitted with an air supply and alarm systems so that if the "corpse" revived, he or she could signal for help.

TOMBSTONE

A tombstone is a stone that marks a tomb, or place where the body of a dead person is laid to rest. *Stone* comes from the Old English word *stan*, meaning "stone," and *tomb* comes from the Greek *tumbos*, "funeral mound."

In ancient times, the dead were often buried under a mound of earth or rocks. Later, people stopped building mounds and buried their dead in the ground, marking the site with a tombstone.

The inscription on a tombstone is called an *epitaph* (from the Greek *epi-*, "on," and *taphos*, another word for "tomb"). Epitaphs range from very simple, with no more than the dead person's name and dates of birth and death, to long essays that tell how much the person was loved, the good deeds he or she did in life, and the honors he or she earned.

In our culture a very popular epitaph is "R.I.P.," short for *requiescat in pace* (Latin for "may he/she rest in peace"). This wish expresses a longing from a time when most people worked many hours a day at hard physical labor, with very few opportunities for rest. It may also express the hope that the dead person's spirit will rest peacefully and not come back to torment the living.

Some Famous and Curious Epitaphs

Here lies one whose name was writ in water.
   —John Keats (1795–1821)

Good friend, for Jesus' sake forbeare
To digg the dust enclosed here;
Bleste be ye man yt spares thes stones,
And curst be he yt moves my bones.
   —William Shakespeare (1564–1616)

Brevet Major General United States
Army born December 5, 1839, in Harrison
County, Ohio. Killed with his entire command at
the Little Big Horn June 25, 1876.
   —George Armstrong Custer

He is not here
But only his pod:
He shelled out his peas
And went to his God.
      —from the tombstone of
          Ezekiel Pease, Nantucket, Massachusetts

On the 22nd of June
Jonathan Fiddle
Went out of tune
      —epitaph for Jonathan Fiddle,
         Hartscombe, England

      In memory of
      Anna Hopewell
Here lies the body of our Anna
  Done to death by a banana
It wasn't the fruit that laid her low
  But the skin of the thing that made her go.
      —epitaph in Enosburg Falls, Vermont

Stranger, tread
This ground with gravity:
Dentist Brown is filling
His last cavity.
      —from the tombstone of a dentist
        Edinburgh, Scotland

27

COFFIN

Coffin comes from the Old French word *cofin*, which comes via Latin from the Greek term *kofinos*, meaning "basket." It's a long way from a basket to a box for holding a dead body, but coffins have been used since ancient times—at least, by those people who could afford them.

Possibly the oldest known coffins were those of the pharaohs and nobles of ancient Egypt, dating as far back as 3000 B.C. These important people were buried in man-shaped containers of stone to protect their bodies for all time. (The Egyptians believed that the soul came back to reclaim its body sometime after death.) The Chaldeans, who flourished in the Near East about 900 B.C., buried their dead in huge clay jars that were built around the body and then baked. In medieval England, the rich were sometimes buried in coffins of lead or iron. But the common people were sewed up in a linen sheet called a "shroud" and put into the ground.

In the United States, *casket* is a synonym for *coffin*. The word *casket* is of unknown origin, a real mystery. When it first appeared in English in 1467, it meant a little box, especially one to keep jewelry in. At some point during the nineteenth century, Americans began using this word to refer to the box in which dead people were placed for burial. This euphemism was probably intended to make people think of the departed person as precious, like fine jewelry.

Coffins and caskets contain corpses. The word *corpse* comes from the Old French *cors*, a misspelling of the Latin *corpus*, meaning "body." Originally (around the beginning of the fourteenth century) the word meant a live body. Then people began referring to a "dead corpse." Finally, they just left the "dead" out, because everyone agreed that a corpse was not living. (We spell *corpse* with a *p* because in the 1300s French scribes put the *p* back in to make the word more like its Latin original. English scribes followed suit.)

An old belief was that at midnight on Halloween the graves would open and the corpses emerge to hold eerie revels in the graveyard. Any living mortal who witnessed this was doomed to die, or at least be stricken with madness.

Does this sound familiar? You've probably seen Michael Jackson's music video "Thriller."

MIDNIGHT

Midnight comes from the Old English *midniht* (from *mid*, "middle," plus *niht*, "night"). The very idea of midnight has a spooky feeling about it. We think of it as a time for magical activities, for we speak of midnight as the "witching hour."

Midnight is the hour when the dead are said to emerge from their graves. It is the time when witches meet in secret to plot wicked deeds, and when sorcerous spells are most effective.

The Witching Hour

People who believe in witchcraft believe that witches can work their magic at any time of day. Why, then, is midnight particularly connected with witchery?

The answer seems to be that when fanatical priests and friars were concocting witch-hunters' manuals in the fifteenth-century, they believed that witches gathered regularly to worship the Devil. Obviously the witches would not meet by day, when they ran the risk of being discovered. They had to carry on their gruesome rituals under the cover of darkness. So, the witch-detecting experts reasoned, the sinister midnight hour was the logical time for the witches' presumed Devil worship.

MOON

The moon moves across the sky like a person on a journey. Every twenty-eight days it appears to be born, grow big and bright, and dwindle away and die, only to be born again out of the blackness, over and over.

With its regular cycle of "birth" and "death," the moon was one of our first means of measuring time. The word *moon* itself can be traced to an ancient Indo-European root meaning "to measure." In Old English this root took the form *mona*, from which our "moon" is descended.

To us, the moon is an "it," but in a number of languages, including German and Old English, the moon is a "he." In French, Spanish, Italian, and other languages descended from Latin, the moon is a "she." This confusion of genders is a reminder that, from some unknown time in the past up to the beginning of the Christian era, men and women worshiped the moon as a very powerful deity.

The Babylonians and the Egyptians worshiped male moon-gods, but the Greeks and Romans worshiped the moon as a goddess. This goddess was called by such names as Selene, Luna, Diana, and Hecate. Hecate has a direct relation to Halloween, for in Greco-Roman mythology she was the patron goddess of witches, the queen of ghosts, and the mistress of black magic.

Even after Europe's peoples stopped (officially, at any rate) believing in the old pagan gods, the superstitious fear of the moon lingered on. Just as people believed night was a kind of anti-day, and the Devil an anti-God, so, too, was the moon an anti-sun, the sun of evil beings who thrived under its chilly glare. It was said that the light of the full moon turned werewolves into their wolf form, and that if moonlight struck you when you were asleep, it could drive you insane. In fact, the word *lunatic* comes from *luna*, Latin for "moon." If you didn't become lunatic, you might be "moonstruck," plunged into deep melancholy and apathy, or sunk in romantic fantasies.

Fortunately, none of these beliefs was true—but if the moon happens to be full on Halloween, turn on your imagination and maybe you'll see a witch floating across it on her broomstick!

SKELETON

Skeleton comes directly from the Greek *skeleton*, "the dried-up thing," the idea being that the bones dried up and remained for years after the rest of the body had rotted away. Since the skeleton is almost permanent, it became a symbol of death early on.

In medieval Europe, a capering skeleton was often pictured leading the "Dance of Death," a procession of men, women, and children; kings, nobles, and commoners; popes, priests, and monks, all headed unwillingly toward their inevitable end. In that period, bubonic plague, known as the Black Death, carried off people by the thousands as it struck again and again. Whole towns were devastated. In some places, only three persons in ten survived. So it is no wonder that the people of Europe were obsessed with death and its symbols.

Science has taken away most of our dread of skeletons; in fact, medical training would be badly handicapped without skeletons to teach future doctors the essentials of anatomy. But most of us would still recoil in horror if we found a skeleton in our bed. And cardboard skeletons decorate the windows of many a house on Halloween to add to the eerie atmosphere of that night.

SKULL

The grinning skull with its gaping nose holes and black, empty eye sockets is a grim, frightening reminder of our own mortality.

The word *skull* was first used in English at the end of the thirteenth century. It was probably borrowed from Danish or Norwegian invaders who settled in the northeast of England. The original Scandinavian term, *skoltr*, seems to be related to the Old Norse word for "bald." So the skull may originally have been "the bald thing." The native Anglo-Saxon word for skull was *braegenpanne*, meaning "brainpan," or *heafodbolla*, meaning "headball."

The Romans called the skull simply *caput*, their word for "head." To be more formal, they sometimes called it *calvaria*, from *calvus*, meaning "bald," in the same fashion as the ancient Scandinavians. The Greek word for "skull" was *kranion*, from which we get the medical term *cranium*. (*Migraine*, a terrible headache that afflicts some people, comes from *hemikranion*, or "half skull," because a migraine headache usually affects only one side of the head.) *Kranion* seems to come from the same root as *keras*, the Greek word for "horn," and its original meaning was probably something like "the hard thing."

Artists during the Middle Ages in Europe often worked skulls into their paintings and carvings as a threatening reminder to sinners that they'd better mend their ways. In much the same spirit, pirate flags a few centuries later bore the insignia of a skull and crossbones to show the intended victims that the pirates meant business.

Sorcerers sometimes used powdered skull or moss scraped from the skull of a long dead criminal in their magical preparations. Strangely, philosophers and seers liked to keep skulls in their studies as symbols of how short a time man has to live. No doubt visitors were impressed by the familiar way in which these learned men handled the ghastly relics.

OWL

To the ancient Greeks the owl, which was sacred to the powerful goddess Athene (goddess of wisdom and protectress of the city-state of Athens), was a lucky bird. To most peoples of those times, however, it was a bird of ill-omen. The Romans feared the owl as a messenger of death and considered it bad luck even to glimpse an owl by daylight. Many American Indian tribes had similar superstitions, which survive in European and American folklore to this day.

The word *owl* comes from the Old English *ule*, which was probably an imitation of the bird's hoot. It may go back to a very old root meaning "to howl." In fact, another Old English name for the owl was *howl* or *howlet*. Many kinds of owls make eerie, moaning, or wailing noises, like ghosts. No wonder people think owls are spooky!

Some people think that owls can turn their heads all the way around, in a complete circle. In reality, this is an illusion. An owl's neck is very flexible, and if you walk around an owl that is perched on a branch, it can turn its head in a complete half circle to follow you. (By comparison, human beings do very well if they can turn their heads far enough to get their chins even with their shoulders—try it!) As you keep walking, the owl snaps its head back in the same half circle—to where it started from. This happens faster than most people can see; so it *appears* that the owl's head has made a complete, uninterrupted circle!

BAT

The word *bat* comes from a Middle English word, *bakke*, whose pronunciation was changed to "bat" in the late 1500s, when Queen Elizabeth I sat on the throne of England and Shakespeare was a boy. There was an older English name for the bat, *reremouse*, from the fact that the bats native to England look like mice with naked, leathery wings. In fact, the name for the bat in many languages means "flutter mouse" or "bald mouse." Bats are not mice, however, and some scientists think they are more closely related to humans than to mice!

Bats are the world's only flying mammals. Some of the big fruit-eating bats that live in the tropics grow to be over a foot long, with a wingspread of nearly five feet, but the bats with which most Americans and Europeans are familiar are small and mouselike.

Some bats eat fruit; some eat flower nectar; a few kinds catch frogs and fish. The vampire bat lives on blood from living animals. But most bats eat insects, which makes them helpful to human beings.

In spite of their useful habits, bats have a bad reputation. In many parts of the world, people believed that the souls of the dead took the form of bats and flew about at night. Probably some of the famous haunted castles of Europe first got their reputations because they harbored numerous bats, which the villagers assumed were malevolent ghosts. In some parts of the world, people believed that the Devil liked to take the form of a bat in order to spy on mortals. In Sicily, people used to burn bats alive to vent their hatred of the Devil.

Witches and vampires were also thought to have the power to turn themselves into bats. Who can forget the evil Count Dracula flaring his cloak and emerging as a bat, the better to enter the bedchambers of sleeping maidens?

Do You Know

In some parts of the world bats are considered lucky. In China and Poland they are good-luck omens. To the Chinese, in fact, the bat stands for long life and happiness. In Britain, some people think that fair weather is coming if you see a bat flying. On the Samoan Islands, in the southwest Pacific Ocean, the natives say that the war god takes the form of a large bat and flies ahead of a war party when he wants it to win. (If the bat flies toward the warriors, however, they will be defeated.)

CAT

Cats have always been mysterious creatures. Even today, millions of people believe that it is bad luck for a black cat to cross their path.

Cats were accused of being familiars—demons in animal form that served as liaisons between a witch and the Devil. People also believed that a witch could take the form of a black cat in order to travel about undetected on her evil errands. Under the guise of fighting the Devil, peasants in France and other parts of Europe burned thousands of cats alive at ceremonies during Lent and on Easter Eve.

Our domestic cats are descended from a small wild cat of North Africa and the Near East, *Felis silvestris libyca*. Scientists think that wild cats began hanging around human dwellings in the Near East about seven thousand years ago when the very first towns were built. People tolerated the cats because they were useful in keeping down the numbers of rodents, but it took thousands of years for cats to become truly domesticated.

Cats were first tamed in ancient Egypt about 2000 B.C. In Egypt, cats were sacred to a goddess named Bast, and they were probably domesticated as temple animals before they began living in people's homes.

Nowhere in the world were cats treated as well as in ancient Egypt. The Egyptians loved their house cats, which they called *miu*. Rich men bought silver earrings to adorn their cats. When a cat died, all family members shaved their eyebrows in mourning. Dead cats were even mummified (you can see cat mummies in museums) to assure them a pleasant life in the hereafter. Quite a contrast with being burned alive!

House cats reached Europe by way of Greece, where they arrived about 500 B.C. The Greeks were mystified by the cat, which they sometimes called "the Egyptian weasel." Ordinarily they called it *ailuros* or *feles*, names they used for the tame polecats (a kind of big weasel) that they employed as mousers. The Romans took over the name *feles*, but by A.D. 100 a new name began to creep in, which in Latin was *catus* and in Greek *katta*. No one knows for certain how *catus* originated, but probably Roman frontier troops picked it up from the Celtic or German tribesmen they were always fighting.

catus –

DEVIL

The word *devil* comes from the Greek *diabolos*, which literally means "accuser" or "slanderer." The idea was that the Devil stood beside people's souls on Judgment Day and reported to God every bad thing the people had done. Later, it was thought that the Devil was God's chief enemy. The belief in a supreme Prince of Evil, far above ordinary demons in power and malignity, goes back far in history.

The ancient Hebrews believed in an archangel of evil whom they called *Satan*, meaning "adversary." But this Satan was not nearly as powerful as God. In fact, he was doing a job that God had assigned him: that of the Tempter, tempting people into sin and punishing them when they fell for his tricks. He could do nothing without God's permission.

The early Christians, like the ancient Hebrews, believed in an Adversary, but they made him much more powerful. Some leading Christian theologians held that the entire world belonged to the Devil, who often seemed to be a jump ahead of God at every move.

It is thanks to the early Christians that we picture the Devil with horns and hooves. When Christianity gradually spread over Europe, the newly converted peoples (many of whom had been converted by force) did not want to stop worshiping their old gods, although they were quite willing to pray to Christ as well. To stop this practice, the Church told the people that the pagan gods were really devils.

One of the most popular pagan gods in the area where Christianity first took hold (the lands around the Mediterranean Sea) was Pan, a god of nature and of herdsmen, who was half man and half goat. Pan had a human head and torso, but the legs and horns of a goat. In other parts of Europe, the peasants worshiped horned gods that were part sheep, bull, or stag.

The Church relied heavily on paintings and statues as visual aids for the common people, very few of whom could read. And so the Devil came to be depicted in the form of the horned gods whom the Church wanted to discredit. Later, the Devil acquired a barbed tail because he had come to be

identified with the serpent who tempted Eve in the biblical story of the Garden of Eden. The Devil's tail was given a barb, unlike that of a real serpent, to suggest the idea of a sting.

Some unknown artist, probably in the twelfth or thirteenth century, had the sinister inspiration of giving the Devil the leathery, angular wings of a bat. The bat wings suggested powerfully that the Devil was a fallen angel, for real angels were pictured with handsome wings like those of eagles.

Nowadays, some people think of the Devil as a suave, handsome, well-dressed man, without the paraphernalia of horns and hooves and tail and bat's wings. In this guise, the Devil has resumed his former role as the Tempter.

Some Other Names for the Devil

People were afraid to refer to the Devil by name, because, if he heard them, he might appear and carry them off. Instead, they used such euphemisms as "The Evil One" and "The Prince of Evil," believing that the Devil would not see through these tricks.

At the same time, to make the Devil seem less frightening, people in almost every country gave him nicknames, such as "Old Scratch," "Old Nick," and "Old Horny." In Scotland he is called "Auld Cloots"—*auld* is the Scottish way of saying "old," and *cloots* refers to his cloven hooves. "The Dickens" was another common nickname. "Dickon" or "Dicken" was an old nickname for Richard, and Richard was a very common name in England in the Middle Ages.

There is also a long list of aliases for the Devil, some of which were once the names of separate evil beings. These are a few of them.

Lucifer (Latin for "light bringer")—a name for the morning star.

Beelzebub (Hebrew for "Lord of the Flies")—originally a god worshiped by a tribe with whom the Hebrews were at war.

Belial (Hebrew for "worthlessness")—the spirit of evil personified.

Mephistopheles—This name first appeared in 1587, in an early version of the legend of Faust, a scholar who sold his soul to the Devil. It really means nothing at all, but it may have been made up from Greek roots by someone who did not know his Greek very well to signify "hater of the light."

Pluto (from the Greek name for "Lord of the Underworld").

Our word *demon* comes from the Greek word *daimon*. To us, a demon is an evil supernatural being, a minor devil. But to the ancient Greeks a *daimon* was a powerful spirit that could just as easily be good as bad. The Greeks believed that everyone had a guardian *daimon* watching over him or her, just as many people today believe they are protected by a guardian angel.

From the most ancient times down to about the eighteenth century, people all over the world believed in demons—some still do! Demons served as convenient explanations for all the bad things in life: falling down the stairs, a headache, a quarrel with a friend, the milk going sour, and so on. Sometimes demons were highly specialized. In Babylonia, for example, people believed there was one demon that caused stiff necks, another for backaches, another for upset stomachs, and still others for every ache, pain, and sickness that mankind could suffer.

About two hundred and fifty years before the Christian era, Jewish scribes translated the Scriptures into Greek. (Greek was then the most important language in the Middle East, and almost everyone understood it.) The Jewish translators, like everyone else then, believed in a multitude of evil spirits, and they used the word *daimon* to cover all of them. The good spirits they called angels, and so today a demon is always an evil being.

IMP

Imp was originally a word used by growers of fruit trees; it meant a young shoot or bud of a plant used in grafting, an art that the Anglo-Saxons called *impian*. (Grafting is a technique that makes it possible to raise hundreds or even thousands of fruit trees or other plants from a single parent.) In time, *imp* came to mean a bud or sprout of a different kind, this time on the family tree, in other words, a child.

When the great European witch-hunting mania got under way in the late fifteenth century, people used the term "imp of Hell" or "imp of the Devil" to designate the kind of petty demon that became the familiar of a witch. By the early seventeenth century, the qualifiers were dropped because everybody knew what kind of an imp was meant. At that time, people took witches and devils very seriously; yet they playfully called a mischievous child an imp, as we do today.

PRANK

No one knows the origin of the word *prank*, but pranks themselves are probably as old as mankind. A prank is a mischievous trick, one that causes annoyance, embarrassment, or worse to its victim. When *prank* first appeared in English, around 1525, it meant a malicious trick, and it has kept some of that meaning. Generally speaking, a prank is funny to everyone but the victim.

Halloween and pranks have always gone together. In the days when America was still mainly rural, boisterous country youths would topple outhouses, soap windows, and hide the neighbors' cows and horses in the bushes. There are even tales of pranksters leading a cow up to the belfry of a church steeple!

Another favorite Halloween trick was to sneak up to a house and fasten a string with a weight on one end—such as a pebble or a nail—to a window. The pranksters would pull the other end of the string, making the weight knock and rattle against the windowpane. When someone in the house came to investigate, the hidden pranksters would shriek like ghosts and frighten the person out of his or her wits.

GOBLIN

A goblin, at least originally, was a household spirit with limited power. Goblins were usually malicious, but they could be friendly if they were treated properly.

The word *goblin* apparently comes from a French word, *gobelin*. This was the name of a nasty local spirit that supposedly troubled a town in Normandy, a province of France. The name came to England sometime in the fourteenth century, about three hundred years after the Normans conquered England in A.D. 1066.

In Shakespeare's time, country folk believed in a being called the "drudging goblin," which would sweep the floors, churn the butter, and do other household chores—if you bribed it with a dish of porridge.

A hobgoblin was a friendlier sort of goblin, more interested in playing pranks on people than in doing harm. The *hob* in *hobgoblin* is an old country nickname for "Robert." So *hobgoblin* really means "Bobby Goblin."

GHOST

The word *ghost* comes from the Old English word *gast*, and originally it had nothing to do with spooks or specters. It meant the life force, the thing you lose when you "give up the ghost," or die. Then it took on the meaning of "breath," which is one of the signs of life. Later, people used it to mean the soul or spirit, the part of a person that is believed to live on after the body dies. But nowadays it means the soul or spirit of a dead person who returns to visit the living for purposes good or evil—all too often evil.

In Europe in the Middle Ages, people believed that ghosts were condemned to haunt certain places as punishment for their sins. A criminal's ghost might haunt the scene of his crime. The ghost of a person who had taken his own life might haunt the spot where he had killed himself. The ghosts of sinful aristocrats (and there were plenty) paced the halls of their castles at night, moaning in anguish.

Sometimes a ghost would appear to a living friend or family member to warn of a disaster or to demand vengeance on someone who had wronged the dead person. A famous example of this occurs in Shakespeare's tragedy *Hamlet*: The ghost of Hamlet's father, the murdered king of Denmark, appears and demands vengeance on his treacherous brother, Claudius, who murdered him.

"I am thy father's spirit," the ghost tells Hamlet. "Doom'd for a certain time to walk the night, / And for the day confined to fast in fires, / Till the foul crimes done in my days of nature / Are burnt and purged away. . . . If thou didst ever thy dear father love . . . Revenge his foul and most unnatural murder." (Act I, Scene 5)

But you had to be very careful about such demands, for the ghost could be the Devil in disguise, tempting you into the mortal sin of murder. In fact, Shakespeare teases the audience with hints that the ghost of Hamlet's father is really the Devil.

Nowadays, cartoons and comic strips picture ghosts as sheeted figures, a tradition from bygone times when people were buried wrapped in a winding sheet, or shroud. We picture two eyeholes in the sheet so that the ghost can see (although, as a spirit, it shouldn't need eyes in order to see). Some ghosts are depicted as loaded with chains, each link standing for a sin they committed during their lives.

In Charles Dickens's (1812–1870) famous story *A Christmas Carol*, the grasping, coldhearted miser Ebenezer Scrooge is confronted by the ghost of his dead partner, Jacob Marley, dragging just such a chain. Marley's ghost warns Scrooge to change his ways or share Marley's fate. Three other spirits, the Ghosts of Christmas Past, Christmas Present, and Christmas Yet To Come, guide the unwilling Scrooge down the path to reform.

Today, ghosts are often portrayed as friendly and helpful instead of angry and vengeful. Casper the Friendly Ghost is a good example. George and Myra, the ghostly friends of Cosmo Topper, and the ghost in *The Ghost and Mrs. Muir* are others. Any self-respecting ghost from the old days would gnash its teeth and rattle its chains in embarrassment!

Apparition is another word for a ghost, the kind of high-flown word beloved by writers of Gothic horror fiction a century and more ago. Actually, it means "appearance," and it comes from a Latin word, *apparere*, "to appear," which is also the grandparent of "apparent" and "apparently."

In the days of King Henry VIII (the first half of the sixteenth century), English speakers were using *apparition* to mean the action of becoming visible. So, they would say things like: "Do you see that pallid form, with its head beneath its arm, take shape where none stood before? It must be the apparition of a ghost." Later, the meaning shifted to the ghost itself.

Another synonym for "ghost" is *specter*, which comes from the Latin word *spectrum* and has its roots in the verb *specere*, meaning "to look at" or "to see." A ghost is something you look at when it becomes visible, even if you don't want to see it.

In modern use, *spectrum* means the whole range of visible colors. It was given this name by the great English scientist Isaac Newton (1642–1727), who was the first to discover the fact that white light could be broken up into a rainbow of different colors by a prism. Newton named this lovely display *spectrum* because it made him think fancifully of the "ghost" of the light.

Look! There's a MONSTER,
a PHANTOM, a VAMPIRE, and
a WITCH riding a BROOMSTICK
with her FAMILIAR to
a late-night CEREMONY!

MONSTER

In the beginning, the word *monster* had no connection with giant size. To the Romans, who gave us the word (in Latin, it was *monstrum*), a monster was any bizarrely deformed human, animal, or even plant.

Thanks to science, it is now known that deformities are caused by something that goes wrong with the development of the embryo or fetus, but to the Romans and other pre-scientific peoples, deformities were caused by the direct interference of gods or evil spirits. People believed that monsters were warnings from the gods that some disaster was about to strike. In fact, *monstrum* comes from another Latin word, *monere*, meaning "to warn." (Our word *premonition*, a sense of impending danger, comes from the same root.)

Since the beginning of time, men and women have created their own imaginary monsters. Here is a chart describing the main features of some of these strange and fearsome creatures.

NAME	PLACE OF ORIGIN	CHARACTERISTICS
Lernean Hydra	Ancient Greece	snaky water monster with seven heads
Minotaur	Ancient Greece	gigantic cannibal man with a bull's head
Sphinx (Greek)	Ancient Greece	winged monster with a woman's head and breasts, a lion's body, and the clawed feet of a bird of prey
Chimaera	Ancient Greece	a hideous creature with the head and forequarters of a goat, a lion's body, and a serpent's tail; sometimes pictured with three heads— lion, goat, and serpent—all breathing fire
Griffin	Medieval Europe	a huge creature with wings of a falcon, a fiercely beaked head, and a lion's body
Wyvern	Medieval Europe	a two-legged griffin or dragon with a barbed serpent's tail

Basilisk or *Cockatrice*	Medieval Europe	a two-legged lizard with the head and wings of a cock; its touch was instant death; its breath was poison; even its look was fatal
Isikqukqumadevu	Zulu Tribe, Africa	a fat, bloated, squatting water monster with a beard; can make itself as big as a mountain; it swallows up unwary people and animals
Izingogo	Zulu Tribe, Africa	baboonlike creature whose ancestors were human; covered with hair, runs on all fours, and has tail, but speaks like human; eats human flesh

Yeti (*Abominable Snowman*)	Himalayan Mountains, especially Tibet	huge, shaggy apelike creature that lives on high mountains and in lonely valleys; smells very bad
Stone Giant	Seneca Tribe, North America	cannibal giant dressed in clothes of stone that cannot be pierced by any arrow or spear
Kappa	Japan	a child-size goblin with a monkeylike face, a turtle's shell, and webbed hands and feet; lives in water and preys on children and animals; has a saucerlike dent in the top of its head, which is filled with water; when the kappa bends over, the water spills out, and it loses its power

Today we don't believe in these particular monsters, but we have created plenty of our own monsters to take their places. Just think of King Kong, Godzilla, Darth Vader, the Thing, the Body Snatchers, Freddy, and countless others. Horror movies, TV, and novels have given us monsters by the dozen. And then there is Frankenstein's monster, perhaps the most famous of them all!

Do You Know

In 1818 a brand-new novel called *Frankenstein* thrilled and horrified readers in England. It was considered so shocking that it was published anonymously, but the author was a young Englishwoman named Mary Wollstonecraft Shelley (1797–1851). She was the wife of the famous poet Percy Bysshe Shelley, and she had actually written her story two years earlier, when she was only eighteen.

Frankenstein, which became an instant best-seller, is an early science-fiction tragedy. Frankenstein, the title character, is a brilliant young scientist. Trying to find a means of bringing the dead back to life, he decides to begin by creating an artificial being out of parts of dead bodies, both human and animal. Since bigger parts are easier to work with, he makes his creature eight feet tall. Once brought to life, it turns out to have more-than-human strength and endurance.

The creature is frightfully ugly. Longing for friendship, it seeks out people but finds that they either run from it screaming with fright or throw stones. Embittered and despairing, the monster begins killing people for revenge, especially the family of its creator, Frankenstein. Frankenstein pursues the monster far out onto the ice of the Arctic Ocean to kill it, but dies of exhaustion. Thwarted in its final revenge (for it planned to kill Frankenstein), the monster delivers a pathetic speech and vanishes into the Arctic night to commit suicide.

Mary Shelley's monster had no name, and he was not described in any detail except as huge and extremely ugly. But in 1931 the American film *Frankenstein* was released, and the monster, played by Boris Karloff with hideous scars and electrodes protruding from his neck, stole the show. The public, infatuated with the nameless monster, called *him* Frankenstein, and the name stuck.

Here is an excerpt from Mary Shelley's original novel.

I started from my sleep with horror; a cold dew covered my forehead, my teeth chattered, and every limb became convulsed; when, by the dim and yellow light of the moon ... I beheld the wretch—the miserable monster whom I had created. . . .

Mary Wollstonecraft Shelley,
Frankenstein; Or, the Modern Prometheus, 1818.

PHANTOM

Phantom comes from the Greek word *phantasma*, which could mean "mere appearance," "illusion," or "image." In time, it came to be a fancy way of saying "ghost."

Phantasma comes from the Greek verb *phainein*, "to show." *Phenomenon* (meaning either something directly observable by the senses or something very unusual), *fantasy* (meaning the creative imagination or something created by the imagination), and *fantastic* (meaning bizarre or strange, or having no relation to reality) are all related to *phantom*.

There is another word, *phantasmagoria*, that was invented in 1802 as a name for a show that was exhibited in London by a clever German named Philipstal. Skillfully using a magic lantern and painted slides in a darkened room, Philipstal made ghosts, skeletons, and monsters appear, grow to huge size, and sink into the floor before the delighted and horrified eyes of his audience. Since the word "phantom" implies something that is only appearance, with no substance, Philipstal's illusions were genuine phantoms.

One of the great horror movies was *The Phantom of the Opera,* made in 1925 and starring Lon Chaney. The Phantom is a homicidal maniac who haunts the subterranean passageways to the Paris Opera House. A former musician whose face is hideously deformed, the Phantom emerges to take revenge on other performers. He dies saving a lovely girl singer from a fire that he has set. (The girl was the only one who had befriended him.) The story was based on a melodramatic and highly improbable novel by a French newspaperman, Gaston Leroux, originally published in 1911. The movie was such a hit that it has had a number of remakes. It has even been made into a Broadway musical.

VAMPIRE

The word *vampire* comes from eastern Europe, like the fictional Count Dracula. It is probably derived from the Magyar (Hungarian) word *vampir*, which may ultimately come from a Turkish word for "witch," *uber*. Why Turkish? From 1526 to the late 1600s most of Hungary was part of the Turkish Empire, and some Turkish words passed into the local language. In fact, the Turks controlled most of eastern Europe, which is where most of the familiar vampire lore comes from, until the late 1870s.

The Turks did not invent the vampire legend. Belief in vampires goes back thousands of years. Some of the oldest writings that have ever been discovered, in ancient ruins in the Middle East, tell stories of bloodsucking monsters that return from the dead to prey upon the living. And doubtless people had been telling similar stories for thousands of years before writing was invented.

The legendary vampire is practically immortal. It can be killed only by sunlight, which makes it crumble hideously into dust; by driving a stake through its heart as it lies sleeping in its coffin during the day; or by shooting it with a silver bullet.

If you can't manage any of these measures, you can still drive off a menacing vampire by holding out a crucifix or wearing garlic around your neck.

There was a *real* Dracula. He was a Romanian prince who lived in the fifteenth century. Dracula was actually his nickname; it means "son of the Devil." His real name was Vlad, and he was usually called Vlad the Impaler from his habit of impaling his enemies—of whom he had many—on sharp stakes. He especially enjoyed feasting out of doors, surrounded by a forest of victims writhing in agony on their stakes. Dracula was indeed a cruel, bloodthirsty monster.

An unknown British author, Bram Stoker, who wanted to write a vampire novel, heard about Dracula through a scholarly friend. He decided to base his fictional vampire on the real Dracula. His novel, *Dracula*, was published in 1897—and the fictional Dracula is still going strong!

Wanted on Suspicion of Vampirism

The best-known vampire in the world is Count Dracula, the chief character in Bram Stoker's shocking nineteenth-century novel. This is what the original Dracula was like.

Appearance: a tall, old man, clean shaven except for a long, white mustache

Complexion: pallid

Nose: aquiline, thin, high bridged, with peculiarly arched nostrils

Chin: broad and strong

Hair: abundant and white; thin around the temples

Eyebrows: white and very bushy, almost meeting over his nose

Ears: extremely pointed

Mouth: cruel, with protruding, sharp, white teeth and very red lips, mostly hidden by his mustache

Hands: broad, with squat fingers, the fourth longer than middle; hair in center of palms; ice-cold to the touch

Breath: offensive odor

Strength: superhuman

Clothing: black

Behavior: courtly and charming

Speech: excellent English, though with a strong accent

Born: fifteenth century

Died: late nineteenth century

If this suspect is sighted in your neighborhood, notify your local horror fan club *IMMEDIATELY!*

WITCH

Witches are as much a part of the Halloween scene as demons, goblins, and ghosts. But witchcraft is even older than Halloween. It dates back to the dim, distant time when we first tried to control the gods and spirits by means of magic.

The word *witch* comes from the Old English *wicce*, meaning "one who practices magic." *Wicce* probably stems from a root meaning "to know" or a similar word meaning "to turn aside." A witch, so people believed, knew how to turn away misfortune, how to bring people things they wanted, and how to harm her customers' enemies (and her own, too).

In Anglo-Saxon times, *witch* could mean a man or a woman. Nowadays it is taken for granted that a witch is a woman, usually old and ugly, and we call a male witch a *wizard*. This word comes from *wise* plus the ending *-ard*. *Wise* comes from an old root meaning "to know," and -*ard* was a kind of ending that expressed disapproval (you'll find it in words like cow*ard* and drunk*ard*). When *wizard* was first used, in the fifteenth century, it meant simply a man of learning. Evidently people then didn't think much of knowledge. Later, it came to mean a man with a very special kind of learning: knowledge of the black arts.

Witches claimed that they could, with the aid of evil spirits or the Devil himself, inflict pain, cause sickness, and even bring death. They could make cows stop giving milk, hens stop laying, and pigs fail to get fat. They could bring plagues on the farm animals and blight on the crops, interfere with butter making, and turn ale sour.

Witches did a booming trade in love potions and charms to attract a husband, wife, or lover for their clients. They also sold highly effective poisons to anyone with a grudge to settle: women with unfaithful husbands, men who wanted to destroy a hated rival, anyone, in fact, with an enemy to get rid of. Sometimes the witch also administered the poison to make sure it brought the desired result.

Most people believed that witches really did have magical powers, but up to the beginning of the thirteenth century many Church leaders taught that witchcraft was nothing but superstition. During the thirteenth century the Church changed its mind and decided that witchcraft was real, and that witches gained their power by worshiping the Devil. Worse yet, Church leaders said, Christianity itself was in danger from a world-wide network of witches, led by their master, the Devil. Zealots in the Church declared a holy war on witchcraft, and the great witch-hunts of Europe slowly got under way. A dreadful period followed.

Anyone could bring an accusation of witchcraft, and thousands of people did, often out of envy or spite. The accused were tortured viciously to make them confess their sins. Sooner or later, most of the accused did confess, even though they were innocent. (Some people really did practice witchcraft, although of course they did not have real magical powers.) After confessing, the "witch" was executed, usually by burning in the public square. (In England witches were hanged, not burned.) Many thousands of people were wrongfully executed as witches.

One famous person tried for witchcraft was Joan of Arc (1412?–1431), a national heroine of France. An uneducated peasant girl, Joan believed that saints appeared to her and told her to raise an army to drive the English invaders from France. (The English royal family claimed a large portion of France by inheritance, and sent a large army to back up their claim.) Joan succeeded brilliantly until the English captured her during a battle. The English brought her to trial as a witch, hoping to discredit the king of France by proving that he owed his successes to witchcraft. Among the "evidence" against her were her visions of the saints and the fact that she wore men's clothing. The English were unable to prove that she was a witch, however, and had to settle for having her burned alive for heresy.

During the peak of the witch hysteria, from the fifteenth century to the end of the seventeenth century, a number of manuals for witch-hunters were written. These books listed all the actions that could be defined as witchcraft and gave lurid descriptions of the witches' rituals. They gave instructions for examining an accused witch, including the methods of torture that should be used, and, most importantly, the manuals furnished a long list of telltale signs that gave a witch away, such as having moles, warts, numb spots, or keeping a pet. The most famous of these witch-hunters' manuals was the *Malleus Maleficarum*, or "Hammer of Witches," published in 1486 by two Dominican friars working for the Inquisition: Jakob Sprenger and Heinrich Kramer. Most of our current ideas about witchcraft come from the witch-hunters' manuals.

One of the last great flare-ups of witch hysteria took place in Salem, Massachusetts, in 1692, when some bored and mischievous girls accused an old black slave woman named Tituba of afflicting them with fits. Fifty-two innocent people were accused of witchcraft. Nineteen of them were hanged, including an unpopular Congregational minister, and one was pressed to death beneath heavy weights before the hysteria ran its course.

🦉 Do You Know

In England and her North American colonies, a quick and easy test of witchdom was "swimming." The suspected witch's left thumb was tied to her right big toe, and vice versa. She was then thrown into a pond or stream. If she were guilty, the witch-hunters said, the water would reject her, and she would float. If innocent, she would sink, and the witch-hunters would pull her out by a rope tied around her middle. Sometimes they waited too long, and the unfortunate woman drowned.

Some Other Witch Words

Necromancer comes from the Greek *nekros*, "dead person," plus *manteia*, "divination." A necromancer was thus someone who could predict the future by calling up the dead, who were believed to have knowledge of things to come. Later it came to mean someone who practiced black (harmful) magic.

Sorcerer is the English form of the Latin *sortiarius*, one who foretold the future by interpreting lots. (The Latin word for a lot was *sors*.) *Lots* were magical objects such as dice, stones, or sticks, or the knucklebones of animals, which were dropped on the ground. A sorcerer could predict the future by the way they fell. Like *necromancer*, *sorcerer* came to mean someone who practiced black magic.

Spell comes from an old Germanic root meaning "tale." A witch's spell is a set of words possessing magical power when uttered.

Warlock comes from the Old English *waerloga*, meaning "enemy," "traitor," or "devil." Today it is a synonym for *wizard*, but some of its older meanings included an oath breaker, a damned soul in hell, a conjurer, and the Devil himself.

BROOMSTICK

It is hard to imagine a witch without her broomstick—but where does the word come from?

Broom was originally the name of a kind of prickly shrub. In the old days, its twigs were used to make a device for sweeping floors. Other kinds of twigs were used, too, such as heather and birch. But apparently the broom plant was so much better for sweeping that its name was given to the tool itself, just as the name "cork" was given to bottle stoppers made of cork.

The old twig brooms were made by tightly tying a bundle of twigs around the end of a stout stick. The word *stick* comes from the Old English *sticca*, which meant exactly what "stick" does today.

Broomsticks had no extraordinary significance until the late fifteenth century, when the notorious witch-hunters' manual *Malleus Maleficarum* was published. The authors of the manual insisted that witches rode through the air on broomsticks to their secret meetings. And that's how the belief began.

FAMILIAR

A *familiar* sight is one you know well. If you are *familiar* with the scores of your favorite basketball team over the last five years, you know them well, too. These are the ordinary meanings of *familiar*. But there is another, more sinister meaning: A familiar is also an evil spirit or demon that serves a witch or wizard.

The word *familiar* comes from the Latin *familia*, which meant "the slaves of a household." (*Famulus*, the root word, was one of the Latin words for a slave.) Later, *familia* came to mean the family as we understand it: a group of related persons such as grandparents, parents, children, uncles, aunts, and cousins.

Since masters and household slaves knew each other well, as did relatives, *familiar* gradually came to mean "well-known" or "well acquainted with."

The familiar of a witch (short for "familiar spirit") was not only well acquainted with her, it was also her hardworking household slave. A familiar had to obey all of the witch's orders and do all her dirty work, and it had to carry messages between the witch and the Devil. The familiar also gave the witch instructions in evil deeds.

Familiars usually took the form of some animal. In much

of Europe, familiars were believed to take the shape of cats, particularly black ones. They could also appear as mice, rats, bats, dogs, crows, owls, and even toads or bugs. In Norway and Finland, familiars often took the shape of flies.

Having a familiar made life easy for the witch, but it could also be dangerous. If a familiar, in its vulnerable animal shape, were injured, its witch or wizard would suffer the exact same injury. If the familiar were killed, its master would die, too. Or so the frightened believers in witchcraft told themselves.

CEREMONY

Ceremony comes from the Latin word *caerimonia*, which originally meant "sacredness" or "awe" or "reverence," and later came to mean the rituals that one followed to show these qualities. When we speak of a ceremony today, we mean a set of things we do to show that the occasion is a special and important one.

Some Halloween ceremonies were originally fortune-telling rituals. One that has lived on to our day is bobbing for apples, although the fortune-telling part of it has been forgotten. Bonfires were originally lit to keep evil spirits and witches away. Dressing up in scary or outlandish costumes was once a way of disguising yourself so that evil spirits would not recognize you. Trick-or-treating comes from an ancient ceremony for pacifying evil spirits by giving them food and drink. All together, they add up to a lively evening.

All that for a little CANDY?
Why not go to a Halloween party instead?
There is one down the street
where they are bobbing for APPLES,
wearing COSTUMES, and
discussing SUPERSTITION.
You'll recognize the house
by the JACK-O'-LANTERNS
in the front yard.

CANDY

Candy comes from the Arabic and Persian word *qand*, meaning "crystallized sugar"—what today we would call rock candy. Actually, *candy* is short for *sugar candy*, the original term in English, which dates back at least to A.D. 1420. English speakers did not start saying *candy* by itself until late in the eighteenth century. At that time the word still meant hard candy; the general word for all kinds of sweet things was *sweetmeat* or *sweet*. The British still observe this distinction, though we do not in the United States.

When trick-or-treating began, people would hand out treats like sweet buns, apples, nuts, and pennies to the children who came to their doors. Candy was a scarce and expensive luxury, too costly to hand out.

About halfway through the nineteenth century, when newly invented machinery made it possible to refine sugar cheaply, the price of candy dropped. Penny candy appeared in the United States in the late nineteenth century. Candy corn was one of the early favorites, along with nonpareils and licorice whips. The first chocolate-coated candy bars—Goo-Goo Clusters and Pearson's Nut Goodies—made their appearance during the baseball season of 1912, in plenty of time for Halloween.

APPLE

The word *apple* comes from an ancient northern European root in a long-dead language, so old that not even the experts can pin down exactly when or where it originated. The original form was probably something like *abl* or *abol*, but over hundreds of years it took on many different forms. In Old English it was *aeppel*. The apple has always been one of the most popular fruits in the world, and it is supposed to be good for you, too. "An apple a day keeps the doctor away," people say. So how did this wholesome fruit come to be linked with the scariest night of the year?

In the mythology of many ancient cultures, including Greek, Roman, Scandinavian, and Celtic, the apple had many magical qualities. It could cure sickness, serve as a love charm, test faithfulness, ensure fertility, make a person immortal, and protect against evil. So it is no wonder that the apple came to be associated with the magical, sorcerous aspects of Halloween.

The apple's main use on Halloween was not to protect against evil, but to tell fortunes for the coming year. Its special talent lay in predicting who a girl's husband would be. One oldtime ritual called for a girl to go alone to her room at midnight, sit down in front of her mirror, and cut an apple into nine slices. As she ate the slices, she looked into the mirror. If the spell worked correctly, her destined husband's face would take form in the mirror, and he would ask for the last slice.

In the British Isles, from which most of our Halloween traditions come, people also played special Halloween games with apples. One favorite was called apple-snapping. To play it, you hung a sharp-pointed stick from the ceiling, high above the floor, and impaled an apple on one end and a lighted candle on the other. Then you set it twirling around. One by

one, the players had to leap up and try to snatch the apple in their teeth without getting burned by the candle. As you can imagine, this game was very dangerous, and people eventually stopped playing it.

Another game, bobbing for apples, is still being played at Halloween parties. It began as a way of predicting the future, and this is one reason why it is played on the spooky night of Halloween.

As far back as anyone can remember, apple-bobbing has been played by children. In the old days before chemical fertilizers and pesticides, apples were usually small and runty, and some children cheated by sucking a whole small apple into their mouths instead of trying to grab a big one in their teeth. Another sly trick was to go for an apple with a stem on it and clamp your teeth on the stem.

The *Macintosh* apple is named for a Scottish-Canadian farmer who found the first one on a seedling apple tree on his pioneer farm in Ontario in 1796. The apples from this tree were so tasty that Macintosh gave grafts from the tree to his neighbors. All the Macintosh apples today come from clones of this one tree. The original tree lived and bore fruit until 1908. It is commemorated by a monument near the spot where it stood.

Russet apples are named for the way their skins turn brown and slightly rough as they ripen. (Russet comes from an Old French word, *rousset*, which means "reddish brown." *Rousset* was also the name of a kind of rough woolen cloth that was used for the clothes of poor country folk.) Russet apples originated in Europe centuries ago.

The *York Imperial* apple originated in York County, Pennsylvania, in the early 1800s and was named Imperial because someone called it "the imperial of keepers," meaning that it kept better in storage than any other apple.

The *Chenango Strawberry* apple is named for Chenango County, in upstate New York, although it originated in Ohio sometime before 1850, and for its strawberrylike shape.

The *Snow* apple is named for its snow-white flesh. It was planted by early French settlers in Canada around 1600 and brought to the United States about a hundred years later. The Snow apple probably originated in France during the late Middle Ages.

The *Granny Smith* is named for an Australian woman who took some apples from home when she moved from the island of Tasmania (off Australia's southeast coast) to the Australian mainland. Before she could eat them all, some of the apples went bad, and she threw them out behind her house. One of the seedlings that sprouted from her dump eventually bore tasty apples that stayed green even when they were ripe. Now they are one of the world's most popular apples.

The *Rhode Island Greening* is usually seen in stores as a big, green apple, although it does turn yellow when fully ripe. It is believed to have originated in the orchard of a Rhode Island tavern keeper who planted the tree in 1748. His name was Green; so there is a double reason for its being called Greening.

The *Grimes Golden* apple originated in West Virginia before 1800. As early as 1804 it was being sold to the traders who went down the Ohio and Mississippi rivers to New Orleans in man-powered flatboats and keelboats. It is named for its color, and presumably for the person on whose farm it originated. The Grimes Golden is one of the parents of the Golden Delicious.

COSTUME

The word *costume* comes from the Italian word *costume* (pronounced co-stoo-may), which means "custom" or "style." A little after 1700, artists and sculptors began to use the word *costume* to describe the outfits their clients wore when they posed for them. It had become the fashion to portray people in the garb of ancient Greece and Rome, whose cultures were supposed to have been the peak of civilization.

Pretty soon, it was not only artists and sculptors who were using the word, but their clients, too. By the next century, *costume* was generally used to mean any particular style of clothing, and also the outfits worn by actors on the stage.

Dressing up in outlandish costumes is an old Halloween tradition that goes back hundreds of years. During the Middle Ages, people sometimes celebrated All Hallows' Day (the day after Halloween) by parading around their churches dressed up as angels, saints, and devils.

Costume parties go back a long time. King Henry VIII of England (1491–1547) was very fond of parties at which he and his nobles and courtiers tripped around in fantastic guises. King Louis XV of France (1710–1774) was another lover of costume parties. He met his famous lady-friend Madame Pompadour (the one for whom the hairstyle is named) at a

costume party where he came dressed as a clipped yew tree,
needles and all! Madame Pompadour came as the goddess
Diana, with a little jeweled bow and arrow that she aimed
playfully at the king's heart to get his attention.

🦉 Do You Know

Masks are often an important part of a costume. The word *mask* comes from the sixteenth-century French word *masque*. No one has been able to trace this word back any further with certainty. But masks themselves go back into prehistory. A painting made by cave dwellers many thousands of years ago shows a sorcerer wearing a deer's mask. Almost certainly this was part of a hunting-magic ritual to attract game animals.

In ancient Greece and Rome, actors wore masks instead of makeup. The Latin word for *mask* was *persona*, from which the English words *person* and *impersonate* also come. (Originally, the actor "impersonated" a god, a handsome young man, or any other kind of character by putting on the mask that went with the role.)

The Romans had another word for *mask*: *larva*. Strangely enough, *larva* also meant "ghost." When naturalists began studying insects in the late seventeenth century, they chose *larva* to be the scientific name for the grub stage because they considered the grub to be a masked or disguised form of the adult insect. And many insect larvae are so pale they remind one of ghosts.

SUPERSTITION

Superstition covers a wide range of beliefs and practices, from the idea that nailing a horseshoe over your door (pointing *up*, of course) brings good luck, to believing that the positions of the stars at the moment of your birth will govern your entire life.

Many superstitious beliefs have their roots in age-old magical practices. For example, many people at least halfway believe that spilling salt brings bad luck. But if you promptly toss a pinch of that spilled salt over your left shoulder, the curse is canceled. People once believed that the Devil was standing behind the left shoulder of the person who spilled the salt, so that the salt was tossed into his face and drove him away. Today, many people superstitiously toss spilled salt over their left shoulder without knowing why!

The word *superstition* comes from the Latin word *superstitio*, which literally means "standing above." The connection with irrational beliefs is impossible to find, although some language experts think that the ancient Romans imagined a person standing over some marvel in amazement or awe. An old definition of superstition is an unreasoning fear or awe of the unknown or the imaginary. Over time, the word picked up other meanings, such as a belief in magic or in things that just are not so.

Some Superstitions from Around the World

(The source of the superstition is in parentheses.)

If you want to drive someone crazy, scrape up the dirt in which he has left his footprints and put it into a gourd. Add two buzzard feathers. Throw the gourd into running water at midnight. (MISSISSIPPI, UNITED STATES)

Knocking on wood keeps bad luck from spoiling your plans. (NORTHERN EUROPE)

The number thirteen is unlucky. (EUROPE, MIDDLE EAST)

If a candle flame turns blue, there is a ghost in the house. (EUROPE)

Blacksmiths can change themselves into hyenas. (ETHIOPIA)

A gambler who plays with dice made from dead men's bones will always win. (INDIA)

When fleas bite more than usual, it is a sign that rain is coming. (BRITAIN)

To prevent ghosts from entering your house, bury camel bones under the door. (INDIA)

If you hear a big spider scrambling about under your bed, it means a witch is coming near. (NIGERIA)

A wife can keep her husband from running away by burying a live horned toad in a jar under her house. (MEXICO)

A child that has teeth when it is born will grow up to be a witch or a vampire. (Slavic countries of eastern and central EUROPE)

You should never bring red and white flowers to a friend in the hospital, for they are a symbol of death. (BRITAIN)

If you wash your car, it is sure to rain. (UNITED STATES, CANADA, BRITAIN)

Sweeping your floor at night brings bad luck, but sweeping it in the morning gets rid of evil influences. (NIGERIA)

Never give a friend a knife or a pair of scissors, or you will become enemies. But you can avoid this if the friend "pays" you for it with a penny. (ENGLISH-SPEAKING NATIONS)

If you try to count the stars, you will get a wrinkle on your face for every one you count. (SPAIN)

JACK–O'–LANTERN

A jack-o'-lantern is a hollow pumpkin with a grotesque face carved into it, and a light inside. Right? Well, if you were a seventeenth-century Englishman, a jack-o'-lantern would be a night watchman carrying his lantern with him. (Remember, those were the days before street lighting; if you didn't carry a lantern with you, you had to find your way in the dark.) Jack was—and still is—a familiar form of John, and it was such a popular name that it came to be a slangy way of saying "man." And so a jack-o'-lantern was really a "man with a lantern."

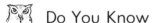 Do You Know

---

The name "John" comes from the Hebrew *Yohanan*, meaning "God is gracious." *Lantern* comes from the Latin *lanterna*, which in turn probably comes from the Greek *lampter*, from *lampein*, "to shine." A lantern is a container that protects a candle or oil lamp from wind and rain while letting light shine through. In the old days, glass was very expensive, so lanterns were usually made of very thin pieces of cow horn. The horn didn't let as much light through as glass, but it transmitted enough to let people see a short distance.

During the Middle Ages, Europeans had a Halloween custom of hollowing out a large turnip, carving eyes, nose, and mouth on it, and lighting a candle inside. This turnip face was supposed to fool demons. Since the turnip was, in fact, a kind of lantern, it, too, began to be called jack-o'-lantern.

The turnip was the standard jack-o'-lantern until explorers brought the pumpkin back to Europe from the New World. Then the pumpkin gradually took over from the turnip. It is much easier to make into a jack-o'-lantern, because it is naturally hollow and filled with seeds that are easy to scoop out. A turnip, on the other hand, is solid inside and pretty hard and crunchy. The pumpkin also has the advantage in size. It takes a *big* turnip to be as large as even a small pumpkin.

The turnip jack-o'-lantern has lingered on in parts of Europe, but in the United States and Canada the pumpkin reigns supreme.

A ghostly custom that was once widespread was to keep a ring of candles burning around a corpse awaiting burial. This was believed to keep demons from entering the corpse and using it for their own purposes. The word *candle* comes from the Old French word *candel*, which comes in turn from the Latin word *candela*. The ultimate root is the Latin word *candere*, "to shine."

The earliest candles, more than five thousand years ago, were made from reeds soaked in melted animal fat. They made a lot of smoke, smelled bad, and gave little light. Later, wicks were invented, and these made candles burn better and give more light. In the Middle Ages the best candles were made of beeswax, but beeswax was always a scarce item and therefore costly. In the eighteenth century it was found that better, and much cheaper, candles could be made from spermaceti, a waxy substance found in the head of the sperm whale. Sailing ships from many nations scoured the seas, hunting the giant whales ruthlessly.

By the 1860s the demand for spermaceti for candles and sperm oil for lamps had come close to wiping out the sperm whales. To the rescue came the growing science of chemistry, for chemists found how to make a cheap, hard wax called stearin out of animal fats. Today most candles—including those that provide the flickering flames for jack-o'-lanterns—are made of stearin or waxes derived from petroleum.

Having fun?
Well, before you go home to bed,
and MOAN, GROAN,
QUAIL, QUIVER, and QUAKE
through a FRIGHTful NIGHTMARE,
just take a minute to imagine
all the INVISIBLE things
that HAUNT Halloween night!

MOAN AND GROAN

    Moan and *groan* are so often used together that we sometimes forget they are separate words and originally had different meanings. *Groan* comes from the Old English *granian*, which meant a low, drawn-out sound indicating pain or suffering, just as it does today. *Moan* comes from the Old English *man*, which originally meant a complaint or lament. In fact, we still speak of a person "bemoaning" his or her hard fate.

And we say things like: "Jack was moaning because he didn't win the competition."

A lament or a complaint is usually more effective if you make it in a sorrowful, suffering tone. So *moan* gradually came to mean almost the same thing as *groan*. There are, however, subtle but important differences between the two words.

A moan is not as deep or harsh as a groan. A moan suggests the eerie sound made by the wind. We never say, "The wind groaned in the trees around the lonely cabin." Nor do we say, "The overloaded truck moaned its way up Three-Mile Hill." (Although the truck's driver may be moaning because of the bad traffic!)

There is an expression, "the groaning board," which refers to a table with a heavy load of food and drink on it. The famous singer Bing Crosby was once called "The Groaner" because of the way he dragged out some of the long notes in his songs.

Ghosts moan in hollow tones—but seldom groan—as they utter their eerie warnings or pleas for help.

Groan is related to the word *grin*, which we think of as a particularly big, good-humored smile, but literally means to draw back your lips so that your teeth show. In fact, the original meaning of *grin* was to make a face in pain or anger. Think of that the next time you see a grinning jack-o'-lantern!

QUAIL, QUIVER, AND QUAKE

Here are a trio of shivery words beginning with *Q*.

The verb *quail* means to lose heart, be discouraged, or shrink back in fear. The word appeared in English around 1400, but nobody knows where it came from. At first, *quail* meant to fade or wither away, and it was used only in reference to plants and domestic animals. "My rosebush is quailing," someone might say.

Later, *quail* came to be applied to the fading away of a person's courage in the face of peril. *Quail* in this sense was very popular among poets and writers from about 1520 to 1650. Then it suddenly fell out of fashion and was hardly used at all for over a century—until it was revived in the early 1800s by the best-selling British novelist Walter Scott. Scott specialized in historical romances, and he loved to use strange, old-fashioned words to give his stories the right "period" flavor. The reading public lapped his books up eagerly, making Scott a rich man and earning him a knighthood.

Nowadays, *quail* is better known as the name of a bird, but the two words are not related.

Quake comes from the Old English *cwacian*, meaning "to shake" or "to tremble." For more than a thousand years it has had a special link with the idea of fear or fright. In seventeenth-century England the religious group called the Quakers were supposedly given that name as an insult because the early Quakers trembled and shook with emotion at their religious services. The Quakers, however, have always called themselves the Society of Friends.

To quiver means to tremble rapidly but without much motion, like a dish of Jell-O when you tap it with a spoon. People can quiver as well as quake with fear. Perhaps they quiver when they are too frightened to quake.

A writer of horror fiction might say, "Jennifer quivered in terror as the sturdy oak door quivered under the blows of the monstrous being that came from the dark crypt beneath the cellar."

Quaking, on the other hand, can be pretty violent, as in the word *earthquake*. "Jeff quaked with fright as the hideously reanimated skeleton stalked toward him, glowing with an eerie green radiance."

The origin of the word *quiver* is not known. The word apparently just sprang into existence sometime during the late fifteenth century, the way *quail* had done earlier. *Quiver* can also mean a case for holding arrows, but this word has nothing to do with trembling. In fact, a bowman who quivers would have a hard time pulling an arrow from his quiver and getting off a shot.

FRIGHT

Fright is a sudden, sharp onset of fear, caused by something alarming. Seeing a truck rushing at you, out of control; hearing a loud, sudden noise behind you; or feeling a set of sharp teeth closing on your ankle in the dark—all these are capable of causing fright. Frightening people—in fun, of course—is a traditional part of Halloween, and it is part of the reason we dress up as devils, witches, and monsters. The word *fright* comes from the Old English word *fryhto*, which came from an even older word, *forht*, "afraid."

Fear comes from the Old English word *faer*, which was derived from an ancient Germanic root meaning "danger." Science tells us that fear is one of the most basic animal instincts. Fear warns an animal that danger is approaching and that it had better move if it doesn't want to get eaten up. We human beings—and we are animals, too—have our share of fear, perhaps more than any other animal, because we alone have imaginations and can think far beyond the present.

We humans fear the unknown. In prehistoric times this may have saved many lives by making people act with caution in new, strange situations. Fear of the unknown also led our distant ancestors to fill the supernatural world with devils, witches, and ghosts—just like the ones we impersonate at Halloween.

NIGHTMARE

Modern psychology tells us that nightmares are caused by anxiety. A hundred years ago doctors pronounced that they were caused by indigestion. But in earlier times, people believed that these terrifying dreams were caused by an evil spirit that they called the Nightmare. (That was the name in English; other languages express it differently. In German, for instance, a nightmare is an *Alpdrucken*, or "goblin squeeze," or *Alptraum*, "goblin dream." The *Alp* has nothing to do with mountains; it is an old German word related to the English word *elf*. The Romans, perhaps fearing to give the evil spirit a name, called it *insomnium*, which also meant "sleeplessness.")

The Nightmare was usually described as a hideous hag who came and sat on the chest of the sleeper, causing a feeling of suffocation and horrifying dreams. (Scholars believe she was one of the forms of the moon goddess.) In some myths she had nine offspring that followed her on her nightly rounds.

Despite the fact that it ends in -*mare*, "nightmare" has nothing to do with horses. The -*mare* is actually an Old English word for a night demon. *Night* itself comes from the Old English *niht*, which comes in turn from a very old root, *nakt*. So ancient is this root that its descendants are weirdly and wildly different. Language experts have great fun comparing such variations as the Gaelic *nos*, German *Nacht*, French *nuit*, Latin *nox*, Swedish *natt*, Russian *noch'*, Spanish *noche*, and so on. Under any of its names, the night can be a time of dread for mankind, for its darkness conceals real as well as imaginary dangers.

INVISIBLE

Invisible comes from the Latin *in-*, "not," plus *videre*, "to see."

Invisible things have always been scary, for you cannot avoid or defend yourself against what you cannot see. A leopard hidden in the bushes is invisible—until it pounces with its deadly teeth and claws! Spirits are invisible, too, except when they choose to appear. Our ancestors feared both natural and supernatural dangers.

Invisibility was one of the most powerful weapons of demons and other evil spirits. Unseen, they could spy on mortals at will and strike at their victims without warning.

Even in these modern, scientific times, we fear the invisible. If you are passing by a graveyard on Halloween night and hear a strange noise coming from nowhere, you will probably jump right out of your skin!

HAUNT

Everyone knows what a haunted house is: a house with a ghost in it. But the word *haunt* originally had nothing at all to do with ghosts. It is the English form of an old French verb, *hanter*, and when it first appeared in English, in the early thirteenth century, it had two meanings: One was to do something habitually; the other meant to hang about a place or a person. We can still say things like: "For months Jeff haunted Bozo's Gym, watching the prizefighters train and wishing he could be like them," or "The third booth in the Sunnyside Coffee Shop was one of this tragic poet's favorite haunts."

In the late sixteenth century people began to use *haunt* to denote what a ghost did when it habitually showed itself at a certain place such as a house where a murder had taken place. Shakespeare himself used it in more than one of his plays. Now it is the principal meaning of the word.

> For God's sake, let us sit upon the ground
> And tell sad stories of the death of kings:
> How some have been deposed; some slain in war;
> Some *haunted* by the ghosts they have deposed. . . .

William Shakespeare. *Richard II*, Act III, Scene 2.

Haunted houses have long been a staple of horror stories. Skilled writers have played all kinds of variations on the theme, creating ghosts that were not only frightening but pathetic, tragic, heroic, and even comical. It is not only ghosts that can haunt a place—demons and goblins haunt houses, too. And on Halloween the whole world can seem haunted.

TIMELINE

*This chart is meant to give readers a general time frame as well as
specific points of reference to topics mentioned in this book.*

Ancient Times

4500	Early civilizations take shape—Egypt in Nile Valley, Sumer in Mesopotamia
3200	The Sumerians invent writing; written history begins
3000	Egypt is united under one ruler, the pharaoh
3000	The Egyptians invent hieroglyphic writing
2800	The Age of the Pyramids begins in Egypt; mummification is a skilled craft
1800	Abraham leaves his home in Ur and wanders west to Canaan and Egypt
1500	Unknown Egyptian priest writes *The Book of the Dead*
1250	Moses leads the Hebrews out of Egypt
800	The Celts emerge as a distinct people
753	The founding of Rome

750–300	The Golden Age of Greek Civilization
500	House cats reach Europe by way of Greece
300	Celtic tribes rule most of Europe from the British Isles to the Black Sea
49	Julius Caesar is proclaimed dictator of Rome for the first time
0	The traditional beginning of the Christian era
100	The height of the Roman Empire; Rome rules much former Celtic territory
200	The Roman Empire weakens
313–325	Christianity becomes the official religion of the Roman Empire
425–450	Angles, Saxons, and Jutes conquer England
430	Church decrees November 1 All Saints' Day; Saint Patrick brings Christianity to Ireland
476	The final collapse of Rome
497–600	The conversion of Britain to Christianity
793–912	Vikings raid much of western Europe
1066	The Normans conquer England, bringing French influence to the English language
1224	Witchcraft is declared a crime in Germany
1233	Pope Gregory IX starts the Inquisition

The Middle Ages

1250	French bishops describe a witches' sabbath for the Inquisition
1431	Joan of Arc is tried for witchcraft and burned at the stake for heresy
1440	Gutenberg pioneers the art of printing with movable metal type
1476	William Caxton prints the first book in English, a romance
1484	Pope Innocent VIII orders the Inquisition to investigate all persons accused of witchcraft
1487	Henrich Kramer and Jakob Sprenger publish *Malleus Maleficarum* ("Hammer of Witches")
1492	Columbus reaches America
1517	Martin Luther challenges certain teachings of the Catholic Church and starts the Protestant Reformation
mid 1500s	Halloween first appears in the English language
1597	King James of Scotland publishes his book *Demonology*, a detailed account of witchcraft
1602	Shakespeare's *Hamlet* is first performed
1604	James, now also King of England, has Parliament pass a new and harsh anti-witch statute; it is the basis for witch trials in England, Scotland, and the American colonies
1606	Shakespeare's *Macbeth* is first performed

The Renaissance

1616–1625	King James begins to doubt witchcraft and exposes some false accusations
1692	Salem witch trials
1712	Last witch trial in England
1764	The first Gothic novel, *The Castle of Otranto* by Horace Walpole, is published
1770–1848	The Romantic Movement; Shelley, Keats, and Byron at work
1818	Mary Shelley's *Frankenstein* is published
1843	Edgar Allan Poe's "The Pit and the Pendulum"
1897	Bram Stoker's *Dracula* is published
1912	The first chocolate-coated candy bars appear
1931	The American film *Dracula* starring Bela Lugosi is released on Valentine's Day
1931	The American film *Frankenstein* starring Boris Karloff is released
1933	The great monster movie *King Kong* is released
1964	The television series "Bewitched" begins
1968	The television series "The Ghost and Mrs. Muir" begins
1978	The American movie *Halloween* is released
1980	The first *Friday the Thirteenth* is released

The Modern Age

SUGGESTIONS FOR ADDITIONAL READING

Avent, Sue. *Spells, Chants, and Potions*. Milwaukee: Raintree Press, 1977.

Aylesworth, Thomas. *The Story of Witches*. New York: McGraw-Hill Book Co., 1979.

Barth, Edna. *Witches, Pumpkins, and Grinning Ghosts*. New York: Clarion Books, 1972.

Bendick, Jeanne. *Scare a Ghost, Tame a Monster*. Philadelphia: Westminster Press, 1983.

Blumberg, Rhoda. *Devils and Demons*. New York: Franklin Watts, 1982.

———. *Monsters*. New York: Franklin Watts, 1983.

Cohen, Daniel. *The World's Most Famous Ghosts*. New York: Dodd, Mead, 1978.

McHargue, Georgess. *Meet the Vampire*. New York: Lippincott, 1979.

———. *Meet the Witches*. New York: Lippincott, 1984.

Petry, Ann. *Tituba of Salem Village*. New York: Crowell, 1964.

Sarnoff, Jane, and Reynold Ruffins. *If You Were Really Superstitious*. New York: Charles Scribner's Sons, 1980.

Simon, Seymour. *Ghosts*. New York: Lippincott, 1976.

Starkey, Marion L. *The Tall Man from Boston*. New York: Crown, 1975.

BIBLIOGRAPHY

A selection of the most useful sources I consulted in compiling this book follows.

ETYMOLOGY

The Oxford English Dictionary. Compact ed., unabridged. Oxford, England, and New York: Oxford University Press, 1971.
   The outstanding reference work in the field of English etymology.
The Oxford Dictionary of English Etymology. New York: Oxford University Press, 1966.
   A useful supplement to the OED.

MYTHOLOGY, SUPERSTITION, TRADITION, WITCHCRAFT, AND OTHER LORE

Ashley, Leonard R. N. *The Wonderful World of Superstition, Prophecy, and Luck*. New York: Dembner Books, 1984.
   An entertaining and quite comprehensive collection of beliefs and tales. No index.
Donovan, Frank. *Never on a Broomstick*. Harrisburg, Pa: Stackpole Books, 1971.
   An entertaining popular history of witchcraft, with extensive and gruesome coverage of the witch-hunts.

Fraser, Sir James George. *The Golden Bough*. Abridged ed. New York: Macmillan, 1951.

One of the great works on ancient religions and their modern survivals; witchcraft, superstition, and folkways. Still cited in current scholarship. One caution: since the original publication date (1922) there have been great changes in the world, and much that Fraser describes has ceased to exist.

Graves, Robert. *The White Goddess*. Rev. ed. New York: Vintage Books, 1948.

A wide-ranging excursion through the ancient mythology of many lands and cultures, elements of which persist in today's Halloween lore and customs.

Kittredge, George Lyman. *Witchcraft in Old and New England*. New York: Russell & Russell, 1956.

First published in 1929, it still ranks as one of the standard sources on witchcraft and related topics. However, it does not deal in any detail with witchcraft in other geographical areas.

Leach, Maria, ed. *Funk & Wagnalls Standard Dictionary of Folklore, Mythology, and Legend*. New York: Harper & Row, 1984.

Originally published in 1949. Another of the great standard sources. A mine of information on a myriad (from the Greek, "ten thousand") of topics. One weak point: the index is limited to peoples, cultures, and places; thus, you can find Karo Bataks (a people living in Sumatra), Helgoland, and Romany Folklore, but not Witchcraft or Hecate, although these topics are buried in a number of places under other headings.

Limburg, Peter R. *Stories Behind Words*. New York: H. W. Wilson Company, 1986.

Modesty forbids the author to praise his own work. See individual entries for Halloween-related words.

Robbins, Rossell Hope. *The Encyclopedia of Witchcraft & Demonology*. New York: Bonanza Books, 1981.

An excellent compendium of the facts. Much attention is given to individual cases of witchcraft (Joan of Arc is one!) and demonic possession as well as to larger topics such as evidence in witch trials and the notorious *Malleus Maleficarum*. Well illustrated (b/w) with contemporary art and reproductions of authentic documents.

Russell, Jeffrey Burton. *Lucifer: The Devil in the Middle Ages*. Ithaca, N.Y.: Cornell University Press, 1984.

————. *Mephistopheles: The Devil in the Modern World*. Ithaca, N.Y.: Cornell University Press, 1986.

For the serious adult scholar, these exhaustively researched works hold a wealth of solid, detailed information. Russell also explores the theological, mythological, sociological, and philosophical ramifications of his subject.

Starkey, Marion L. *The Devil in Massachusetts*. New York: Alfred A. Knopf, Inc., 1949 and several later editions.

A dramatic, moving, and well-documented account of the Salem witch hysteria.

INDEX